DEATH AND DYING
EDUCATION

Death and Dying Education

by Richard O. Ulin

National Education Association
Washington, D.C.

Note

The opinions expressed in this publication should not be construed as representing the policy or position of the National Education Association. Materials published as part of the Developments in Classroom Instruction series are intended to be discussion documents for teachers who are concerned with specialized interests of the profession.

Library of Congress Cataloging in Publication Data

Ulin, Richard Otis.
    Death and dying education.

    (Developments in classroom instruction)
    Bibliography: p.
    1. Death—Study and teaching—United States.
I. Kelley, Robert, 1944–   II. Title.
BD443.9.U6U45   155.9'37'071073   77-12278
ISBN 0-8106-1816-8
ISBN 0-8106-1815-X pbk.

CONTENTS

216810

1. Why Death and Dying Education

'Tis a vile thing to die, my lord, when men are unprepared and look not for it.

Shakespeare

In recent years, death has made its debut in education. Why should schools concern themselves with death? Don't students have enough to do learning how to live? Are youngsters of school age really old enough and have they lived long enough to face problems of life and death? Is it healthy for them? What useful purpose is served by forcing or even encouraging them to think and think hard about either their own death or the death of other people?

Why focus students' attention on the experience of dying, on the wide variety of ways people approach and meet their end? Are or should young people be interested in aging and the elderly? Why ask them to study funeral rites or even to experience a funeral? What purpose is served by leading them to inquire into the nature of grief or to contrast their culture's mourning practices with those of other cultures? If they do, will this kind of inquiry and experience only open wounds? Can it actually help to avert or ameliorate wounds to come?

Is the current American interest in death and dying merely a reflection of our morbid curiosity? Do the media already provide us with more than adequate coverage? If they do not, are overburdened schools in a position to take on yet one more responsibility? Even if they do have the time, are schools the proper place and are teachers the most appropriate persons we can find to provide young people with the kind of learning experiences they need in an area as sensitive as death?

These are some of the questions which this book addresses on a subject the writer believes will soon be of wide educational concern. Though itself long overdue and hardly yet decided, the debate on sex education will have to move over for debate on another once taboo topic—death. Now that mortality has burst into the arena of public discussion, we are becoming aware that children and adolescents are keenly interested in death, that they have already acquired both conscious and unconscious attitudes towards it, and that they are variously informed, uniformed, and misinformed about it, just as they are about sex. In schools which deal with the real rather than a make-believe world, in schools where young people think about what they can make of their lives, one of the decisions curriculum builders must make is how the classroom can deal with death. Teachers and school administrators cannot act as though death and public concern about it do not exist. If they decide, for whatever reasons, to try to exclude death from the classroom, to minimize students' cognitive and emotional contact with the facts of mortality, this is a decision which they should make deliberately. On the other hand, if they choose to admit death to the classroom, to deal with it in a conscious and even a systematic way, then this, too, is a decision which should be made with all due care since it involves a myriad of collateral decisions and has, perhaps, profound consequences. From one point of view, however, the decision may not need to be made at all by teachers and school administrators. It may actually be made for them. If schools as public institutions cannot, in fact, insulate themselves from vital issues in the public forum, classrooms will probably be forced willy-nilly to deal with death, so strong is the current concern with it.

Why is the public interest in death as intense as it now is? Why the spate of books and articles in the popular press on suicide, on care of the terminally ill, on abortion, on euthanasia, on cremation and burial, on funeral costs and practices, on the right-to-die as well as the right-to-live? In 1970, *Psychology Today*[1] published a questionnaire, "You and Death," and the magazine was deluged with

30,000 returns. Four years later, the *Reader's Digest*[2] for the third time printed "Light, Like the Sun," an article describing the relative virtues of burial and cremation, and the magazine received thousands of requests for reprints. Across the country in formal and informal discussion groups, adults of varying ages, educational backgrounds, and religious persuasions have riveted their attention on problems of aging, death, and dying.

Some see this preoccupation as only a passing popular fad. However, the enormous scholarly and semischolarly interest the subject has generated in the last two decades would seem to indicate otherwise. In increasing numbers, sociologists, psychologists, philosophers, lawyers, the clergy, doctors, and nurses have turned their professional attention to problems which death poses. Strange as it may seem, though persons have been aging and dying as long as there have been people, it is only in recent years that gerontology and thanatology have developed as areas of systematic study. If death and taxes, as the old saw goes, actually are the two things one can count on in life, it is indeed surprising that both serious and public attention to death has been so long in coming. It can hardly be by accident or by oversight. Publishers have always had their eyes on profits, and scholars are always looking for subjects. This lends credance to the theory that the delay in demand and the absence of concerted public attention on death are attributable to some kind of conscious or unconscious avoidance behavior.

Sigmund Freud felt it necessary to appeal to people to admit death into their consciousness. But since Freud's day the world has been wracked by war and terrorized by violence, afflicted by famine and threatened with atomic holocaust—most of it, if not experienced, at least witnessed by millions on newsreels or television. Small wonder that Americans today are acutely aware of their mortality. Small wonder that we and our students have an interest in death and how to cope with it.

Even under ordinary circumstances, people sense they are living in the presence of death. As the only members of the animal world conscious of their own mortality, human beings except in rare situations have never relished the prospect of dying, the extinction involved in the state of nonbeing. Most of us struggle against the concept as well as the fact. In an effort to exorcize ourselves of the problem, most of us have chosen to deny death itself or at least to deny its finality, and in the process we have invented immortality. Yale psychiatrist Robert Lifton stresses the fact that in all cultures all people have found it necessary to establish a connection between themselves, their past, and their future. Some solve the problem by inventing an immortal soul. Others see themselves living on in their children or in their group, their tribe, or their nation; others, through their accomplishments. In an interview with Jean Stein, novelist William Faulkner once said of his own creative efforts: "This is the artist's way of scribbling 'Kilroy was here' on the wall of the final and irrevocable oblivion through which he some day must pass."[3]

To see oneself as immortal in any one or all of these modes may make the prospects of dying easier for some people. But none of them has provided or is ever likely to provide a final solution to the problem. "John Smith not only wants to live forever—he wants to be forever *John Smith*."[4] Freud called the belief in a future existence "the oldest, strongest, and most insistent wish of mankind."[5] The famous Polish anthropologist Bronislaw Malinowski demanded to know, "Am I going to live or shall I vanish like a bubble?"[6] What we have always feared most is total annihilation, the obliteration of our identities. Not so many years ago in the United States, religion could comfort us, but some no longer find reassurance in the promises of redemption and resurrection.

Many of us have tried to sweep death under the rug. Witness the euphemisms we have created for it: When people "pass on," they are "laid to rest" before they pass through the "pearly gates." Witness our increasing search for the modern-day Fountain of Youth—the use of cosmetics and rejuvenation regimes of all types. Witness the way so-called "life insurance" salespersons and the Defense Department treat dead people, be they soldiers or civilians, as actuarial statistics. Certainly movies and TV depict their fill of death, but they turn it into a dramatic illusion. And when death actually does come near us, when those close to us are dying, we see to it that they are removed from us, taken to hospitals and nursing homes where special functionaries care for the dying and later dispose of the corpses. With our sanction, these institutions may cremate the corpse; or they may embalm it and make it more lifelike than when it was alive, and then carry out the interment.

While most of us try to find solace in one or more of the conventional models of immortality, the more imaginative among us strike out in other directions. With a perfectly straight face, the National Academy of Engineering announces that we are about to solve the problem of aging, and death will then come only through accident.[7] Obviously the optimistic spirit of the American frontier lives on and so does our unshakable faith in science. There are many who seriously believe that in the lifetime of this generation we will have learned how to freeze our bodies and then years or generations later revivify them. If we can really land on the moon and on Mars, if we can actually transplant human organs, make babies in test tubes, and crack the genetic code, what makes the science of cryonics so farfetched? At the same time, more and more of us, particularly the young, are putting their faith in psychic research, in breakthroughs in extrasensory perception, in seances, astrology, and witchcraft. In *The Immortalist*, Alan Harrington fairly shouts that it is time for man to shed his "cosmic inferiority complex," to come clean about his heretofore disguised longing and "go after what he wants, the only state of being he will settle for, which is divinity."[8] Our only salvation, as Harrington sees it, lies in medical engineering; "the time has come," he says, "for men to turn into gods or perish."[9]

If one cannot accept Harrington's call to arms, one may still agree with Erich Fromm when he says: "The state of anxiety, the feeling of powerlessness and insignificance, and especially the increasing doubt about one's future after death represent a state of mind which is practically unbearable for anybody."[10] And even if one finds Fromm's assessment an overstatement, at least one must recognize that this is an age of anxiety and alienation, that death is everywhere at hand, and that our lives can become richer only as we come to terms with death. "Coming to terms" with death, as with almost anything important, is a matter of education and this education cannot begin too early. To reach the conclusion that death and dying education is important and should be provided for children in their early years does not necessarily mean, however, that schools are the proper place for it. Nor does it solve the problem of what kind of death and dying education is appropriate at what ages. These are but two of the critical questions that the following chapters address.

11

2. Are the Schools the Proper Place?

> Men fear death as children fear to go into the dark; and as that
> natural fear in children is increased with tales, so is the other.
>
> Francis Bacon

Given their already overcrowded agenda, one might question whether the schools really should concern themselves with yet one more subject area, however significant or pervasive the subject. Various public interest groups would make the schools responsible for every facet of a child's education. Schools, of course, cannot accede to such pressures. They must set their own priorities, recognizing that other institutions may be better equipped than schools to provide for learning in some critical areas. One might well ask whether the family, peer group, church, and media cannot singly or together provide youth with all the death and dying education they need. The answer, I suggest, is both yes and no.

As is the case with sex, the questions children ask parents about death and dying, their own and others', make many parents uncomfortable. Consequently, they may evade the questions or, by partially informing, succeed only in misinforming. On a highly charged issue, one on which children need straight answers and also encouragement to work through their feelings, parents are often least able to provide that help. Some parents have used Santa Claus, a relatively harmless myth, as well as the psychologically destructive Bogeyman to help control their offspring. Some parents when asked by surviving siblings why a little brother or sister died, have provided as an explanation that it happened because God loved the child and wanted him or her in Heaven.

Some young people may find in peer-group situations the forum they need to work through their anxieties, but peer groups vary enormously and they are often highly unreliable sources of information. As Robert Kastenbaum has shown, young children have always ritualized death in their games. When children today "all fall down" in Ring Around the Rosy, according to Kastenbaum they actually are re-enacting the effects of the Black Death in medieval times. The "It" in games of tag Kastenbaum traces to the touch of death.[1] And how many generations of American children have shouted "Bang, bang, you're dead!" in games of cops-and-robbers and cowboys-and-outlaws? As some psychologists maintain, this kind of ritualistic play may be therapeutic, but it cannot be expected to provide the serious information and experience children need if they are to begin to accept and finally come to terms with mortality. Neither play nor teenage talk, then, is likely to provide the answer.

Though ministers, priests, and rabbis have written some of the most incisive and useful materials published for young people on the subject of death, religious institutions themselves vary widely in the degree of enlightenment they show on the subject of death, particularly where children are concerned. Then, too, not some but *all* children need good education, and it is unrealistic to think that more than a small fraction of young people would be reached if religious organizations were the only sources of death education. Many demoninations take doctrinaire positions on such issues in death education as abortion, euthanasia, and the after-life, to name only a few. Religious perspectives on these issues and on others obviously should be considered, but all children, whatever their religions affiliation, have a right to a broad spectrum of information and to an awareness of conflicting viewpoints. Perhaps the school, then, is in the most favorable position to provide this kind of coverage.

It is certainly true that young people are exposed to print and nonprint media that deal extensively with death. At every turn readers, listeners, and viewers are assaulted by violence, homicide, suicide, war, and both natural and unnatural catastrophes. Many recent books, comics, magazines, newspapers, radio, TV, and films all feature people facing and meeting death, sometimes singly and sometimes in casts of thousands. The problem with death and dying education via the media is not one of quantity but of quality. For all their verisimilitude, for all their instant coverage and wide-screen impact in living color, the media have not replaced the firsthand experience earlier generations had with death. On the contrary, they actually anesthetize young people to death and contribute to its unreality. As a consequence, one of the primary tasks of enlightened death and dying education is to counteract media misinformation and enable young people to distinguish specious from truthful media treatment.

Family, church, peer group, and media all add to whatever first-hand experience young people have with death, but neither singly nor together do they provide youth with the objective and comprehensive kind of education they sorely needed. The school, our only societal agency with access to all children, has as its major objective helping young people understand life's problems, one of which is death. The school, therefore, seems to be the logical and perhaps the only feasible locus for this kind of learning experience.

Nevertheless, one might argue, and many undoubtedly will, that however urgent the need, because schools could do the job is not sufficient reason to ask them to do so. Over the years, we have seen the schools move beyond the three R's and beyond the bounds of the traditional disciplines to include sex education. Is it now time to add death and dying education? Or will death and dying education be one more onerous burden on an already overburdened school curriculum? Will it overtax the carrying capacity of a system that many feel is already unable to fulfill its primary responsibilities? Are schools already too busy educating for *life* to concern themselves with *death*?

It is this writer's contention that that is not the case. By and large, the kind of death and dying education programs suggested in the following chapters would not replace existing curricular offerings. They would be fused with and add another dimension to them. They would sharpen, clarify, and provide a base for currently taught subject areas. In some instances, death and dying programs might provide new content, a new subject matter of gripping current interest to students, a vehicle through which teachers might teach more effectively many of the cognitive as well as the affective skills they now teach through more conventional subject matters.

The recent history of death and dying education in the schools seems to bear this out. In every course or unit of death and dying education which the writer knows about or has information on, students appear to have been highly involved and enthusiastic about what at least they felt they were learning. This may not be proof, but it strongly suggests that objectives were being met, that meaningful education was taking place. A few examples at both the college and the high school levels are cases in point. At the University of Minnesota, students, both majors and nonmajors, regularly oversubscribe Robert Fulton's course "The Sociology of Death," the aim of which he says is "to bring a new perspective to death, to show that it is a natural, and to counteract some of the euphemistic devices our society uses to hide death and dying."[2] One of Fulton's education students said that as a result of the course, "I got to the point where I could look at death as a natural function of life." So affected was he by the experience, he went on to draw up a high school course on the subject. At the University of Maryland, Daniel Leviton found that in his "Health Education" course, the only topic to rival sex was death.[3] The unit's popularity, he feels, is due to the rare opportunity it afforded students "to ventilate their fears about death."[4] At Yale in the spring of 1975, so popular was James Carse's course "The Meanings of Death" that 275 undergraduated competed for the 20 places it offered.[5]

The growing demand for death and dying courses in secondary schools also provides strong evidence that in some form the subject is appropriate at this level too. In 1975 some 400 junior and senior high schools discussed death and death-related subjects in one-day workshops, minicourses, English, science, and social studies units as well as in semester-length courses. Glenrock (Wyo.) High School teaches a course called "Death,"[6] South High School (Minneapolis, Minn.) one called "Death Education," Norton (Mass.) High School one in "Death and Old Age," Shaker Heights (Ohio) High School in "Death, Dying and Old Age," and Scarsdale (N.Y.) High School in "Philosophy of Death."[7] In Amherst, Mass., Robert Kelly and Paul Lengieza, social studies teachers, include a death course in their elective program; both students and parents are enthusiastic about the course, and the teachers use it to probe other facets of American culture. At other schools, health educators and science teachers also report successful use of death units as means to their particular ends. In sum, at a time when large numbers of students claim to find school irrelevant and a bore, it would seem derelict of us not to explore the possibility that some kind of formal instruction in death issues might help us energize already existing curricula.

As for the claim that schools are too busy offering education for *life* to take on *death* education, it is a basic thesis of this book that no such dichotomy exists, that death is an integral part of life, that in the struggle to understand life one must make an effort to understand death and the process of aging, as well as birth and the process of growing, that only through coming to terms with death can young people come to terms with life. If this premise be granted, it seems the schools have no choice but to include death and dying education in their curricula.

3. What Should Be Taught?

> Everything has been written which could by possibility
> persuade us that death is not an evil, and the weakest men as
> well as heroes have given a thousand examples to support this
> opinion. Nevertheless, I doubt whether any man of good sense
> ever believed it.
>
> François de la Rochefoucauld

If there is to be death and dying education in the schools, these
questions must be asked: What kind of death and dying education?
What shall it consist of? What should its contents be? What form
should it take? These are questions which, of course, will have
different answers for different grade levels, different answers for
various kinds of communities and various types of students. Suggestions are offered in chapter 7 as to how teachers might take these
variables into account; this chapter explores the wide spectrum of
possibilities the subject offers, the range of questions it opens for
students to study.

Why does death exist? The first question, and one of the most
perplexing, is of what purpose, if any, death serves. Theologians, of
course, offer a variety of religious explanations; but, setting aside
metaphysical convictions and speculations, we can ask, What biological, sociological, and psychological functions does death have?
Is life, in general, viable without death? Is human life possible
without the invariable death of *all* things? Without the invariable
death of *humans?* If so, in what ways would life be different if it
were not for the fact of death? Would we, as humans, see life
differently and would we live our lives differently if death were not
the invariable as well as the expected end? If the date of our death
were predictable, would it make a difference? If means were found
to postpone death or to increase, possibly double, our life spans,
how would our lives change?

Depending on our answers, what would happen to the world's
population? To our natural resources and our life-support system?
To the quality as well as the quantity of human life? These are questions which students at any age can study with profit. In the course

16

of such study, they are bound to enlarge their understanding of themselves, of humankind, and of the natural world. While working at their own level of skill and understanding, students can use the tools of the biologist, the geographer, the demographer, and the psychologist. Death as a subject and the questions it spawns can provide a natural and arresting interdisciplinary focus for learning.

What is death? Certainly one of a school's functions is to provide information, to help students answer answerable questions. A more important task, however, is to nourish students' natural curiosity and stimulate them to ask questions, both answerable and unanswerable. The great breakthroughs, societal and personal, come only when persons question what they or society have heretofore taken for granted. This makes "Why does death exist?" a good question for young people to deal with. For the same reason, they might well ask, "What is death?"

The self-evident answer is that death is simply the absence of life. But even if we are forced to accept this kind of circular reasoning, the answer, we have begun to discover, is not all that clear-cut. Scientists argue heatedly as to where to draw the line between organic and inorganic matter. Closer to home, at what point does a human life begin and at exactly what point does it end? These are hardly academic questions. One of the crucial issues of public policy today is the right to avert or abort or terminate life. Critical ethical and legal decisions are at stake, and in the long run the public, preferably an informed one, will have to make them.

One of the places that can generate informed and objective discussion on these matters is the school. And at some level of conceptualizing, they are matters of concern to young people of all ages. Secondary school students, ready or getting ready to vote and to procreate, may be wrestling with questions of contraception and abortion. Others, turning to vegetarian diets, may be concerned with our right or the necessity to destroy animal life in the interest of human sustenance. Younger children, on the other hand, may be readier to learn the differences between animals and inanimate things, the distinction between sleep and death, the irrevocability of death, and the naturalness of the birth–life–death cycle. Learned at an early age, these concepts can become an integrated part of their intellectual and emotional equipment and can serve as the groundwork on which more sophisticated later development can be built.

How should one respond to death? Whether or not they are aware of the situation, teachers often have students in their classes who have recently been bereaved, who may be preoccupied, even obsessed, with the loss of a brother, sister, parent, relative, or friend. Even if a school were concerned with only the intellectual growth of young people, this would be reason enough for it to provide some help to students who at least temporarily are unable to handle their studies. Fortunately most schools are also concerned with the social and emotional development of students, and those that are not at least recognize that their success as academic institutions depend to some extent on how well students can resolve their personal problems. It, therefore, behooves all schools to set up some crisis intervention machinery, some kind of counseling or referral agency to which students in distress can and will turn for help. Cases of bereavement often fall into this category.

Classrooms themselves, however, can be helpful as they can also be damaging. At times, the fact of a child's recent loss—and the pain of it—burst into a classroom when no one, not even the bereaved, is ready for it. At other times, the fact becomes apparent in more subtle ways. But in any event, it takes a sensitive and prepared teacher to handle the situation constructively. It calls for a teacher who has worked through some of his or her own problems with death and who knows something about the way the death of loved ones may affect young people. What may also be helpful is if the class itself or previous classes have provided the bereaved student's classmates with the kind of death and dying education which makes them better able to relate to the bereaved. The same kind of death and dying education in schools may also enable the bereaved student to cope more adequately with the loss.

Is it ever right to take a human life? As children's attitudes toward death develop, so in a reciprocating way do their attitudes toward depriving others of life. From the time children play ''Bang! Bang! You're Dead! with every assurance that the dead will arise, to the time they are old enough to own firearms and join the armed services, they are in our schools and are concerned with killing, particularly with the killing of human beings.

They ask many questions very early, and few of us every answer those questions with any finality: When, if ever, is it right to kill? Is homocide ever justifiable? Under what circumstances? In the act of killing, do humans ever surmount themselves and become as gods?

Are there unspeakable provocations, such as being raped or tortured, or seeing those we love raped or tortured, which warrant homicide? Is self-defense, or the defense of others, justification for killing? Under sufficient physical or mental duress, are we to be excused for killing? Should the Nazi underlings or the Charles Manson followers have been exonerated? Does society have the right to punish those who kill? If society has such a right, what offenses warrant capital punishment? Who makes the decision? In some instances, is it merciful to terminate another person's life or at least not take available steps to prolong it? Whose decision is this to make? At what point does the welfare or life of a social order take precedence over the life of an individual member? What makes war and participation in it justifiable? Is it natural, inevitable, or right for one community (family, tribe, nation, or race) which feels its life threatened by another social order to kill in order to assure its own existence?

These are all questions which in some form people at almost any age can and should deal with. All of these questions are important for secondary school students, but students at that level will find them more meaningful if they have had the experience in previous years of dealing with some of them in forms appropriate to their earlier levels of maturation. Certainly third-graders are not ready to debate the pros and cons of euthanasia or abortion, but they are ready to begin thinking about when, if ever, it is right for one person to take another's life. That kind of thinking and dialogue in schools can promote intellectual development, and there is also some evidence to indicate that they can accelerate, as Lawrence Kohlberg defines it, the moral development of students.[1] As students tackle the relevant, concrete, controversial issues of death and dying, they can be engaged (in the best Deweyite sense) in active thought, in inquiry learning, in learning to apply the scientific method in problematic cases. They should also, at all ages, be engaged in moral discussion and moral reasoning. It takes, of course, a giant step to move from moral discussion and reasoning to moral action, and one has no right to assume, or perhaps even expect to see concrete evidence, that classroom attention to these issues will produce demonstrable changes in students' in- and out-of-school behavior. One can hope, however, that when students subject to scrutiny some of the values to which they have previously subscribed without question, the process will lead to clarification, adjustment, or confirmation. Teachers who seek to transmit to young people a set of unquestioned traditional values, who are trying to pass on our consensual values through what Lawrence Kohlberg calls "a bag of virtues,"[2] may find the process unsettling. Those who see their role as educators who stimulate rational, critical, or reflective modes of valuing will probably find it exciting.

Is suicide a human right? Another topic which should find its way into some stage of death and dying curriculum in the schools is that of suicide. It certainly is a question for teenagers insofar as, between 1960 and 1973, suicide rates in the 15–24-year-old bracket have more than doubled.[3] In a course he gave at the University of Maryland, Daniel Leviton found that of his 309 students, six had already made a suicide attempt and seven said they had or were then contemplating it.[4] But apart from their own death wishes, all students are regularly exposed in the media to cases of suicide, many of them spectacular; and many of them have had personal experience with the suicide of someone close to them. As young people explore the problem, at one stage or another, all sorts of interrelated legal, ethical, psychological, and sociological questions will rise. Is suicide murder? Is it now and has it always been a crime in all societies? If as humans we have the right to life, liberty, and the pursuit of happiness, do we also have a natural right to die, the right to choose the time and even the manner of our own death? Is suicide an act of weakness or is Dostoyevsky's Kirilov right when he says, "Whoever wants supreme freedom must kill himself. He who dares to take his own life is God."?[5] Does a person's life, and hence his or her death, belong to that person alone or also to God or to society? Is suicide always tragic? Must it reflect a distorted mind or an intolerable situation? What sets of circumstances are conducive to suicide? How can they be ameliorated? What signs are there of an incipient suicide? What steps are appropriate in forestalling the act? How much of our "ordinary" behavior can be construed as suicidal? Are only individuals or are groups capable of suicidal behavior?

These are only a few of the questions about suicide which students can deal with. They are not easy questions and they are bound to raise anxieties, but that is no reason to avoid them, but rather deal circumspectly with them. A teacher has no more reason to avoid discussing suicide with students out of fear that it may prompt them to the act than he or she has to avoid discussing murder, rape, violence, theft, or income tax evasion. Suicide is a fact and one of which students are well aware. What is needed is to remove it from the taboo list so they can find out what the data show, recognize their own current attitudes towards it, wrestle with other viewpoints, and then establish their own personal and rational position. This is a process in which an informed teacher can be helpful.

Can we prepare for the death of a loved one? Is it harder to die ourselves or to witness the onset of death in someone we know and love? It is the rare student who at some time in his or her schooling has not had intimate contact with the dying and death of a loved one, and the experience may vary from unpleasant to excruciating. Immediate contact with anyone who is dying brings home to us our own vulnerability, the inescapable fact that we, too, are dying and will die. When the dying person is also someone we love and someone we see with some regularity, the pain becomes greater and dealing with our emotions even harder. Wrapped up in what Kübler-Ross and others call "anticipatory grief"[6] over our imminent loss are feelings of pity, anger, and even revulsion. Even when we recognize them, these are not easy feelings to handle, particularly when they are directed toward someone we love or with whom we are close. It is, therefore, perfectly natural and human to avoid contact with a significant other who is approaching death.

Whether death education can make the experience any easier is, of course, problematical. Students who are already in the throes of anticipatory grief or of actual mourning are perhaps too emotionally involved to be supported significantly, but for students who have not yet had the experience the preparation may later prove helpful. And certainly classmates who have some understanding of the gravity as well as complexity of the situation can make it easier for a student while he or she watches a loved one die.

What do you say to someone who is dying? Should you avoid talking about it? What can you do to be helpful? No two cases are the same, but enough is known now to help those emotionally involved to be somewhat more comfortable in the presence of dying. Many who have had death education attest to the fact that dealing with the situation "academically" left them with a clearer understanding of their own feelings, a perspective on the feelings of the dying person, and hence a greater ability to cope.

In what ways can death education better prepare young people for the actual loss of a loved one when it does occur? As children differ in age, maturity, stability, and life experience, of course they have different needs when the crisis comes. We are never really "ready" for death, and obviously no previous education can hope to eliminate the trauma, but appropriate preparation can at least minimize the shock and hasten recovery from it. Death education can serve as an antidote to our death-denying society and to the myths and fantasies it transmits. At all ages good death and dying education may at least provide young people with vicarious experience on a relatively unemotional level as well as enough intellectual understanding of the fact of death to enable them to cope more adequately with the situation when it does occur.

After the age of five, as Maria Nagy shows,[7] even young children who do not yet believe in the inevitability of death, particularly their own, are ready to recognize that death, when it happens, is final, that no one recovers from it. One of the difficulties that people of any age often have in moving through the usual stages of grief over the loss of a significant other is that they have learned this only at a shallow intellectual level at a period in their development when they should have learned it fully and deeply. The grief they then experience later in life is more painful and more extended and harder for them to work through. Adequate death and dying education in the early grades, experiential as well as academic, working with plants and animals as well as reading and discussing, can lessen this pain. This kind of education can take place without violating religious convictions parents hold and wish their children to hold, and it can remove some of the myths which parents and the culture have foisted on children in their misguided concern to protect them from the unpleasant fact of death.

This kind of preparation, particularly through literature, can proceed through the middle years of schooling, and at some point in secondary school young people should be introduced in an intellectual way to what grief means. They can learn some of the things Kübler-Ross, Feifel, Kastenbaum, and others have discovered about the mourning process. They can learn how the bereaved often experience shock, disbelief, denial, a sense of guilt or relief, confusion, deprivation, anguish, depression, and anger before working eventually into acceptance and integration of the loss into their lives.

Such knowledge can help students understand and support classmates and others who have suffered loss. It may also make their own later grief more understandable and thereby less alarming and more bearable. Knowing what "grief-work" must be done before one can surmount the loss of a loved one, they are more likely to accept the mechanisms our culture has invented to help us with that work. They are more likely to be ready to play a healthy role in making funeral arrangements, preparing the body, writing obituaries, notifying friends and relatives, disposing of possessions, etc., all activities which are painful but which may make the wound heal faster, prevent delayed grief reactions, and preclude later maladjustment. Particularly since the social upheaval of the Sixties, young people resent being sheltered and have sought out personally relevant, meaningful experiences and have welcomed confrontation with their basic problems. In this climate, they are readier than previous generations of students to study death and, when it comes to them and others, to meet it with healthier reactions and more realistic behavior.

Death-related concerns. There are other questions and problem areas teachers might choose to include in a death and dying education program. Though important in their own right, these questions may not carry the same emotional loading for students and so can offer a change of pace and sometimes a necessary release in tension. For example, in a country in which 50 percent of those who die do so intestate, it is obvious that students also need to be educated to the necessity for making out a will in good time. They need to learn the possible consequences of not doing this, and they need to know how to go about doing it properly. One other means of providing for one's dependents that students should understand is life insurance. Before the day comes when they face the pressure tactics of insurance salespeople, students should learn what insurance can and what it cannot do, what kinds of policies are appropriate at what times in one's life and under what conditions, how one can be ill-insured, underinsured or insurance-poor. At some point young people should also become acquainted with the rights of hospital patients, the functions coroners and medical examiners perform, the reason for autopsies, the need for and uses of a morgue, the nature of funeral options and the value of choosing one early, the possibilities of donating organs to the living, and the cost and paperwork which death occasions.

Another critical area to which a course might well address itself is the problem of growing old in America. So crucial is this problem that the next chapter is devoted entirely to its place in the death and dying curriculum.

4. Aging in America

Do not go gentle into that dark night. Old age should burn and rave at close of day; rage, rage against the dying of the light.

Dylan Thomas

In designing school experiences, teachers and other curriculum builders generally try to gear these experiences to the physical, emotional, and intellectual levels of the young people they have in mind. Some curricula, particularly those in biology, health, and physical education, recognize that young people are and should be interested in their own maturing growth processes, not only in their past and present but also in their future development. Students learn how children are conceived, how they are born, and how they pass through childhood and adolescence into manhood or womanhood. They become aware of the successive stages of human physical growth and of the kinds of physical activity appropriate for them. They may develop some recognition of normal emotional growth, of what it is to mature psychologically in our society. This education, however, is truncated prematurely. What students gain little recognition of is the fact that to grow and mature is also to age, that the moment we start living we also start dying. Certainly young people are—and should be—most concerned with their present stage of development and their immediate future, but their education should also enable them to set these stages in a perspective of the total life process. This calls for more interest and more concern than schools now pay to what happens when people move into middle and old age.

In varying degrees societies have always found the elderly a problem, and our own technological one finds it increasingly so. While there is little evidence to indicate that human longevity or the maximum life span has increased any since antiquity, there is more than ample evidence that the mean life expectancy has increased dramatically (e.g., it rose from 10 years in ancient Rome to 55 years in 1929–31, to 70 years today). In spite of war's ravages, industrial and automobile pollution, workplace hazards, and the like, through eliminating disease and retarding the degenerative processes, science and our declining birth rate are altering the age structure of the American population dramatically. We are an aging society. In the 1900–70 time span, the proportion of our population over 65 has more than doubled, from 4 to 10 percent, and prospects are for a continued increase.

Though we should have been ready for it long ago, the realization of what this transformation in age structure will mean has dawned on us only recently. At a macro-level it obviously presents enormous political, economic, educational, and social welfare problems. For thirteen years the U.S. Senate Special Committee on Aging has advocated that a National Institute on Aging be set up in the Public Health Service, and so, too, did the White House Conference on Aging (1961 and 1971), but not until 1974 did such an institute actually come into being. Now at long last we have a national clearinghouse and a recognized funding agency to foster and conduct biological, medical, and behavioral research on the process of aging. Universities have been quick to react to this new interest in aging. Encouraged by the dollars that research is now being offered by private and public agencies, many universities have set up interdisciplinary departments and institutes to study gerontological problems. Perhaps we can anticipate a belated interest in academic circles in the problems of aging to match that which academics have long devoted to the problems of early childhood and adolescence. Our history of neglect in this field would seem to be paralleled only by our equally long neglect and refusal to recognize the build-up in our environmental pollution problems.

As with most societal problems, corrective action and education will be necessary at the micro- as well as the macro-level, not only in universities and at upper echelons of government but in elementary and secondary schools and in formal and nonformal programs of community action at the grassroots level. Without adequate research and political support, this grassroots action will be uninformed and ineffective; without testing and feedback from programs in action, universities and governmental bodies will find themselves operating in a land of make-believe. Constant communication and interchange between the micro- and macro-levels are, therefore, a *sine qua non* if we are to deal successfully with the accelerating problems of aging in our social order.

In particular, what can the schools do? First of all, beginning in the elementary grades they should make every effort to eliminate misleading stereotypes of what it means to grow and become old. Imbedded in our books, in teacher and student talk, in the everyday language we use, are reflections of the anti-age bias of our youth-oriented society. We know how textbook stereotypes can foster racism in the schools and how they can help determine our culture's attitudes toward sex role differentiation (e.g., that little girls are gentle, keep clean, and grow up to be good housewives, mothers, secretaries, and nurses while little boys are aggressive, get dirty, and grow up to be professional athletes, scientists, and surgeons). The same effort we now expend in schools on erasing these damaging stereotypes we should also exert to erase the stock figures of middle and old age, of people who past thirty begin losing their creativity, their mental and physical capacities, and become conservative and reactionary, interested only in material acquisition and upward mobility and then in their twilight years settle back to enjoy retirement, knitting, shuffleboard, their illnesses, their grandchildren, and their pensions.

From preschool picture books to the literature they read in high school, students learn how good grandparents act and so are socialized into the role they themselves are supposed to play when they, too, reach the age. They learn that "You can't teach an old dog new tricks," that to be young is to be beautiful, that old people are serene and complacent. They learn that old people lose their physical and mental capacities as body and brain degenerate, that they no longer desire or enjoy sex. They labor under the delusion that old people, despite physical pain and economic dependency, enjoy their "senior citizen" status and actually relish enforced retirement and membership in the "Golden Age" Club. As stereotypes often do, these age stereotypes give off an aura of invariability and inevitability. Based as they are on half-truths, they also have the power to close out options and become self-fulfilling prophecies. As a result, despite other possibilities, most of us actually become the old people of our youthful images.

Few of us get to know old people other than our own grandparents. The nuclear family and our early-retirement economic system make them practically invisible to us. Small wonder then that young people see age as a biological process that ostracizes and degrades a person. Aware of the physical decline of older people, our students focus on it, exaggerate and overgeneralize it, unaware that many old people crave and also have a great capacity for mental, social, and spiritual growth. Old people, too, adopt these attitudes since they are contagious. Perhaps we are only as old as we feel, but it is at least equally true that we are only as old as young people think we are. One thing schools can do about age stereotyping is to introduce students to the idea that although aging is a universal process, it proceeds differently with different people, depending both on the person and on his or her social circumstances. This is an idea which would probably be commonplace among the young were it not for the fact that in our society the elderly are socially isolated.

Given the current invisibility of our over-65 population, it is only through a conscious educational process that we can make youth aware of the enormously diverse capacities and potentialities of this expanding age group. With this awareness will also come the realization that aging, because of our cellular construction, necessarily involves deterioration but that the process is not unmanageable. Through public policy and personal action we can exercise a considerable degree of control over how it takes place. One of the school's obligations, it would seem, is to develop in young people not only a consciousness of this fact of life, but also an ethical sense of their responsibility to take both personal and public action. With such knowledge and attitudes, young people are more likely to manage their own aging advantageously and to make life more liveable for the elderly they know intimately. As citizens they may also work to provide intelligently and humanely for the elderly segment of our society.

As young people become aware of what physiological changes to expect as people age and as they come to comprehend the social, economic, and psychological problems our elderly face, they are less likely to avoid both the elderly and their problems. As the veil of invisibility lifts, young people will come to appreciate what it means to old people to lose their memory, at least their immediate memory, to move into a minority group with lowered income, lower social status, and inferior self-image, to suffer job discrimination and the indignities of dependence, to adjust to loneliness and retirement, that is, to suffer at an advanced age what often amounts to an identity crisis. One social critic questions "how long a society that exiles its old folks can preserve its continuity with the young."[1] Young people prepared in school with knowledge of what it means to age and be old in our society, reasonably armed both cognitively and experientially, are more likely to take what steps they can to narrow the growing generation gap.

If children are to acquire this knowledge and these attitudes, they will need to do so gradually, beginning in their earliest school years and continuing in a variety of subject areas through secondary and postsecondary education. Units in social studies and literature courses would seem to be best for dealing with the social and psychological aspects of aging, while biology courses could handle the more specifically physiological problems. In high schools with broad elective programs and at the college level, entire courses, some of them multidisciplinary, could be devoted to the process of aging in America. To provide some experimental base, these courses and units might well include visits to senior centers, hospitals, and nursing homes. Elementary schools could devise other programs like Foster Grandparents to bring young children and older people together to their mutual benefit. In high school, students could learn simultaneously about the past and what it is to be old by working on oral history with retired townspeople. Eliot Wigginton, teacher and editor of the *Foxfire* books,[2] has shown how much young people can learn by working with village elders in a northern Georgia community. The idea would seem to be equally applicable in an urban setting. As another teacher relates, old and young people in South Boston, as well as those in Rabun Gap, Ga., can learn much from each other by putting together the story of a community's past.[3] Still another example of a successful old-young program is a 1976 film series staged at the Senior Center in Amherst,

Mass. Together secondary students and senior citizens first viewed and then discussed the issues involved in twelve classic films dealing with perennial societal concerns (e.g., sex, money, crime, fashions, and love). Out of the interchange, young and old not only learned more about the issues but each group developed a healthy respect for the other's perspective, or perhaps more importantly, for its variety of perspectives.

5. Cross-Cultural Perspectives

Who is a wise man? He that learns from all men.

Talmud

Historians, anthropologists, and sociologists have described for us how other people in other places, times, and circumstances have faced age, death, and dying. It would seem only reasonable that some acquaintance with the variety of options which others have developed can help us as Americans bring our own options more sharply into focus and can suggest to us possible alternatives. Knowing how people in other social contexts relate death and childhood, death and religion, and death and socioeconomic status can help us recognize and assess the concepts of death we hold and our own ways of handling the problems of aging and dying.

One can see a star better by not looking directly at it. Similarly, we may be able to see our own social order more clearly by examining other societies, some of them far removed from us in time and space. In our own relatively sophisticated technological society, whatever our intents or declarations, most of us tend to deny death and to patronize our elders. Just how much we do so becomes apparent by contrasting our attitudes to those of one African tribe, the Akamba. As the story goes, a young tribesman once returned from a long journey outside of the country and reported to the council of elders. The chief thanked him saying, "You have seen much. You are old and we are but children. You have made us older than we were. But you are older still, for you have seen with your eyes what we have only heard with our ears." To the Akamba, age means not the passage of time and deterioration but the potential for accumulating skill and knowledge.

The questions that surround aging, dying, and death are universal human questions, but the answers various cultures have arrived at are obviously not the same. Even among Americans, homogenized as we may seem to be, Catholic, Jews, and Protestants all differ in their outlooks on death, what it means, how it is to be approached, and what is to be done when it occurs. At one time ethnicity appeared to be on the wane in the United States, but in recent years ethnic pride has been rekindled and with it old world customs have been renewed. Vying with the dominant "Yankee" or Madison Avenue modes we see distinctively Polish, Italian, Chinese, Japanese, Greek, German, and Latin American approaches to life and death. Students should learn how our American subcultures variously answer the questions of death and dying. Such understandings help develop self-awareness and can make working and living together easier. For the same reasons, students should also learn how more distant and more exotic cultures have dealt with the same questions.

Students will want to know many things. How does a death-affirming society, in contrast with a death-denying one like ours, deal with problems of life, aging, and death? What approaches do the Buddhists, Taoists, and Confucianists take? What about people who worship nature or ancestral spirits? Eskimos and the American Indians? What prompted the ancient Egyptians to bury live slaves and wives as well as weapons and food with their dead? Why do some Tswana tribes in Southern Africa bury their dead under the floor of their houses? Why do the Chinese and the Basutho make a hole in the roof of the house when someone dies? Why do some groups stage banquets or perform dances or wear black? Why do some destroy, cannibalize, drown, cremate, or bury their dead? Why do others preserve or beautify the corpse? As primitive or exotic as some of these practices may appear to us and our students, they not only reflect the way various people see life and death, but they also attest to the importance people everywhere attach to death as a part of life.

Whatever their rites and customs, social groups have always gone beyond the minimum procedures necessary to dispose of their dead. Preburial and postburial rituals for the deceased generally reflect a whole culture-complex and an outlook on life, and they generally serve a need for the living as well as perform a function for the dead. Properly performed, they serve as a rite of passage to admit the deceased to the land of the dead. They may also save the living from misfortune or unwelcome ghostly visits. On the one hand, socially sanctioned rites such as wailing and self-laceration may prove debilitating to survivors. On the other, such death rites often help release tension among survivors when the dreaded event occurs and help them come to grips with its reality and finality. They may help survivors deal with their own death wishes, their guilt feelings, and their ambivalence toward the deceased and his or her dying. They may also serve a social purpose in bringing the group together again after its unity has been shaken by the event.

In some elementary schools across the country, teachers are now introducing children to anthropological ideas and even helping them learn to use anthropological tools. In learning about other people in other lands and in other times, children are learning not only what these people grow, what they export and import, and who their friends and enemies are, but also what and how they think, how they bring up their young, conduct rites of passage, deal with the infirm, the indigent and the aged, conceptualize death and dispose of their dead. Call it geography, history, anthropology, sociology, or philosophy, it is through such interdisciplinary study and cross-cultural understanding that young people come to glimpse themselves—their own social order as well as the wider world. In so doing, they also learn a way of learning. That way of learning can begin in the elementary grades, which readily lend themselves to such interdisciplinary pursuits. It can then continue, although it takes some engineering, at the secondary level, where schools operate within a more highly disciplined rubric.

Even in conventional English, social studies, and foreign language courses, students can learn how other people face death and dying, how they answer such questions as: What does it mean to grow old? How does one cope with age, even enjoy it? What obligations does one have to the elderly? Why do we die? Why do we die when we do? How does our life on earth relate to our death? Can we live in ways that will prepare us for death? Is belief in an afterlife necessary for peace of mind in the present life? Is it helpful? These are questions which our students do and should ask—perhaps not outwardly or of us, but they are the kind of touchy questions which schools should deal with and which they can often handle most expeditiously and with least emotional trauma in a cross-cultural context.

6. Literature and Death Awareness

> Sooner or later all things pass away and are no more. The beggar and King, with equal steps, tread forward to their end.
> Thomas Southerne

The ultimate justification for including any curricular offering in a school program is whether or not it promises to help students better understand themselves and their world. And however strong the current "back-to-basics" movement, many of us continue to believe that the liberal arts actually do serve to liberalize students and the humanities help to humanize them. Working on this assumption, teachers of death and dying courses should make sure they take advantage of the special contribution which the arts, and particularly literature, can make toward the achievement of their ends. As literary critic Louise Rosenblatt says, "There is an even broader need that literature fulfills, particularly for the adolescent reader. Much that in life itself might seem disorganized and meaningless takes on order and significance when it comes under the organizing and vitalizing influence of the artist." The comment rings equally true if one were to substitute "much that in death" for Rosenblatt's phrase "much that in life." For all of us, adults as well as adolescents, no aspect of life cries out for order and significance with quite as much urgency as death does.

The power of literature as a social force has been well documented. Witness the impact of Voltaire or Dickens or Harriet Beecher Stowe. *Candide, Oliver Twist,* and *Uncle Tom's Cabin* provided molds into which thousands of individual readers poured their shapeless ideas and emotions. In each case the net result was personal revelation as well as powerful social action. When readers enjoy a genuine literary experience, they, along with the author, perform a creative act. They do not merely read *about* an experience, they actually live *through* one; and the kinds of growth and insight which this experience produces is of a very different order from that which follows when readers simply acquire new information. This is not to say that the artist has a corner on the truth market, but that through the medium of the poem, the play, or the novel the artist's vision can penetrate readers in areas and with an intensity which the historian, sociologist, and psychologist cannot hope to reach. It is also true that though insightful, the artist's vision is necessarily selective and partial. Alerted and moved by literary experience, however, readers will seek to re-examine themselves and their world and will then reach out to the more comprehensive information only the social sciences can provide.

Literature can make an impact on any age. Therefore, at whatever grade level death and dying education begins, literature should be included. From the child's earliest years there is a wealth of material, and the teacher's main problem is to select the stories, plays, and poems that appear most appropriate and then decide how to use them. The options are so vast that here we will only mention a number of works which experienced teachers say they have used successfully and also name a few others which we feel can be used with profit.

Perhaps the most difficult ages for which to select appropriate books are the earliest years. At the prereader and beginning-reader stage, roughly to age eight, children vary widely in the degree of exposure they have had to death and dying. These disparities in life experience, depending on their cultural and personal circumstances, make one uneasy about prescribing books in general. Then, too, parents as well as educators disagree, often sharply, as to how early it is healthy for children to learn about death.

In a now classic study she did in 1948 with children aged three to ten, Dr. Maria Nagy found that children are concerned with three basic death questions: What is it? What makes people die? What happens to people after they die? She also found that children pass through three different stages of awareness: from three to five they deny death as a usual and final event; from five to nine, they recognize that people do not return to life from death but still reject the idea that it happens to everyone and will happen to them; and only after ten do they accept death's finality as well as its universality.

Eulalie Steinmetz Ross, formerly Supervisor of Storytelling in the New York Public Library and an authority on children's literature, believes that for the young child up to age eight (usually the third grade) "there is little need in his spring-green world for an understanding of the dead," and she recommends avoiding books that deal explicitly with death. She suggests, instead, concentrating on those which will help provide a child with a kind of emotional security that will enable him or her later to handle problems of dying and death as they arise. Consequently, she restricts pre-grade three reading to perceptive picture books and readers dealing with family relationships, love, God, and the natural world. Books on the family which she strongly recommends are Robert McCloskey's *Blueberries for Sal*, Charlotte Zolotow's *One Step, Two Step*, Margaret Wise Brown's *The Runaway Bunny*, Hardie Gramatky's *Little Toot*, Else Minarik's *Little Bear's Visit*, Helen Buckley's *Grandfather and I*, and Thomas Handforth's *Mei Li*. For friendship she recommends Taro Yashima's *Youngest One*, Loni Slobodkin's *One Is Good but Two Are Better*, and Leslie Brooke's *Johnny Crow* series. God and the natural world she finds well handled in Florence Mary Fitch's *A Book About God*, Margaret Wise Brown's *A Child's Good Night Book*, Janice Udry's *A Tree Is Nice*, Leo Lionni's *On My Beach There Are Many Pebbles*, and Robert McCloskey's *Time of Wonder*.

There can be no quarrel with the quality of the books Steinmetz Ross suggests, but this writer, along with Marsha Rudman and other experts on children's literature, disagrees with Steinmetz Ross in what we see as her overly protective approach to younger children. Many children, aged eight and under, we feel, have already experienced death and dying in their lives and are, therefore, ready to do so in literature. Books like *Annie and the Old One, Old Arthur, Grandma Didn't Wave Back, Nana Upstairs and Nana Downstairs,* and *Across the Meadow* depict old age truthfully, "telling it like it is." They include the wrinkles and the pain and the loneliness, and they help youngsters understand aging and how to relate to the elderly. Books like *The Old Dog* or *My Grandpa Died*

Today, The Magic Moth, and *A Taste of Blackberries* can help them understand and cope with death itself.

Funerals may be particularly hard for children, but books about animal funerals may help, for example Margaret Wise Brown's *The Dead Bird,* Mildred Kantrowitz's *When Violet Died,* and Judith Viorst's *The Tenth Good Thing About Barney.* Three books about the death of a loved child and how a funeral helped make the event bearable are John Coburn's *Anne and the Sand Dobbies,* Virginia Lee's *The Magic Moth,* and Doris Smith's *A Taste of Blackberries.* These books also deal sensitively with the problem of what happens to people after they die.

For older children, those in upper elementary and middle school, the choice of books widens as does the range of problems they deal with. In *Grandma Didn't Wave Back,* Rose Blue describes the pain Debbie feels as she watches her grandmother turn senile. In Norma Mazer's *A Figure of Speech,* 13-year-old Jennie in the face of her parents' insensitivity, stands by her incompetent but fiercely independent grandfather until his death. E. B. White in *Charlotte's Web* and William Armstrong in *Sounder* describe the death of animals and the grief it causes. In Patricia Windsor's *The Summer Before* and Doris Smith's *A Taste of Blackberries,* young people learn to cope with the death of a dear friend and the guilt feelings that follow. Several perceptive novels deal with the death of a sibling, among them two we've previously cited, *Anne and the Sand Dobbies* and *A Taste of Blackberries.* A third is Scott O'Dell's *Island of the Blue Dolphin,* in which a 12-year-old girl, left alone on an island, not only surmounts the death of her 6-year-old brother but also her urge to kill the wild dogs she holds responsible for it.

Most plentiful are books concerned with the death of parents. In Carol Farley's *The Garden Is Doing Fine,* Connie insists on telling her dying father the truth even if it hurts. She finds herself grief-stricken by her father's illness but at the same time guilt-ridden by her yearning for a return to normality in her own life. In Vera and Bill Cleaver's *Where the Lilies Bloom,* Mary Call actually buries her own father secretly, after wishing him dead, in an effort to keep herself and her siblings out of the poorhouse. Luke, in Mildred Lee's *Fog,* grows up fast after his father's fatal heart attack. The loss of a mother is the subject of two highly emotional novelettes, William Armstrong's harshly realistic story *Sour Land* and Vera and Bill Cleaver's *Grover.* The latter is also a moving story of suicide, as are Norma Mazer's *A Figure of Speech* and Crystal Thrasher's *The Dark Didn't Catch Me.*

The world of imaginative literature obviously offers much in the field of aging, death, and dying to youngsters in the elementary and middle schools, but the fare is even richer for students in secondary school, many of whom are ready for anything on the adult shelves. So rich, in fact, are the possibilities that here we suggest only some of those which have already elicited favorable student response.

At Glenrock (Wyo.) High School, from her experience teaching a death course, Judith Hawkinson recommends the following books: William Blinn's *Brian's Song*, John Donovan's *Wild in the World*, Nancy Garden's *Loners*, Khalil Gibran's *The Prophet*, John Gunther's *Death Be Not Proud*, Norma Klein's *Sunshine*, John Steinbeck's *The Red Pony*, and the anonymously authored *Go Ask Alice*. Poems she finds particulary useful are: William Cullen Bryant's "Thanatopsis"; Emily Dickinson's "Because I Could Not Stop for Death," "The Funeral," and "Devotions XVII"; Thomas Gray's "Elegy in a Country Churchyard"; Nancy Priest's "Over the River"; Mary Riley Smith's "Sometime"; Dylan Thomas's "And Death Shall Have No Dominion"; and Henry Vaughan's "They Have All Gone into the World of Light."

Hawkinson's choices are those which she herself enjoys teaching, and ultimately every teacher must do the same. What follows is a selected list compiled from syllabi of death courses taught in many schools.

> James Agee, *A Death in the Family*
> Edward Albee, *The Sandbox*
> Jean Anouilh, *Becket, or the Honor of God*
> Richard Bach, *Jonathan Livingston Seagull*
> John Barth, *The Floating Opera*
> Robert Bolt, *A Man for All Seasons*
> Pearl Buck, *The Good Earth*
> Willa Cather, *Death Comes to the Archbishop*
> Stephen Crane, *The Red Badge of Courage*
> Thomas Dooley, *Dr. Tom Dooley, My Story*
> T. S. Eliot, *Murder in the Cathedral*
> William Faulkner, *As I Lay Dying*
> Paul Gallico, *The Snow Goose*
> Ernest Gann, *The High and the Mighty*
> William Golding, *The Lord of the Flies*
> Mark Harris, *Bang the Drum Slowly*
> Nat Hentoff, *I'm Really Dragged but Nothing Gets Me Down*
> John Hersey, *Hiroshima*

Herman Hesse, *Steppenwolf*
Nikos Kazantzakis, *Zorba the Greek*
Norman Mailer, *The Naked and the Dead*
Carson McCullers, *The Heart Is a Lonely Hunter*
Arthur Miller, *Death of a Salesman*
Erich Segal, *Love Story*
Leo Tolstoy, *The Death of Ivan Ilytch*
Dalton Trumbo, *Johnny Got His Gun*
Evelyn Waugh, *The Loved One*
Thornton Wilder, *The Bridge of San Luis Rey*
Tennessee Williams, *The Rose Tattoo*
Paul Zindel, *The Pigman*

For nonfiction materials on death and death-related subjects, the teacher should see the Bibliography. Those which appeal to students, as distinct from those which are more appropriate for teachers, are so indicated. This report also lists useful audiovisual materials, films, filmstrips, slide-tapes, and cassettes.

7. The Teacher: Preparation and Qualifications

> Children are educated by what the grown-up is and not by his talk.
>
> C. G. Jung

How brash does one have to be to teach a course or a unit in death and dying education? Brash, indeed, if by death and dying education one means to instruct students in how they ought to age, cope with their own aging and the aging of others, how they ought to prepare for their own death and the death of others, how they should handle bereavement and the bereavement of others, how they should see death in its relationship to life. To teach in such a prescriptive way one would need a pedestal, or at least a lecturn, a sense of omniscience, and a degree of moral assurance many persons do not have. But if by death and dying education one means rather to expose young people in an unthreatening way to some of the facts about death, aging, and dying in our society, to introduce them to a variety of perspectives from other cultures and from artists, philosophers, sociologists, psychologists, poets, and novelists, and most importantly, to help them sort out their own thinking on the subject, then one need not be brash at all.

If one defines good teaching as helping students to learn things which are important to them, then teachers can prepare themselves to teach death and dying education. However, if a teacher only enjoys teaching in areas where he or she has knowledge and students do not, in areas where there are definite answers, in which the facts speak for themselves, then such a teacher will not enjoy teaching death and dying education. If a teacher is uncomfortable when the subject matter touches students' feelings deeply—and in death classes teachers may have to confront these feelings—then such a teacher will be uncomfortable in a death and dying education classroom. If a teacher feels that schools are places society designs exclusively for the cognitive development of young people, that moral and ethical concerns belong more properly in the family and church, then such a teacher should not try death and dying education. If a teacher has been trained in a traditional academic discipline and now finds his or her professional satisfaction from working entirely within that discipline, then such a teacher, too, is likely to be uneasy with death and dying education.

On the other hand, if a teacher sees him- or herself as a learning facilitator, if he or she is at ease in an area where no final answers exist, where he or she is not an authority but rather a fellow learner, where both the teacher and students are emotionally involved, where their emotions actually constitute part of the subject matter, and where disciplinary lines are blurred, then such a teacher may find death and dying education an exciting and rewarding experience.

How much and what kinds of knowledge does the death and dying education teacher need? The answer depends, of course, on what level the teaching takes place and how extensive it will be. The teacher who plans to conduct a third-grade class needs to know different things from those the university professor or high school teacher should know. It makes a difference whether one plans to teach a full-fledged course or a small unit, whether one plans to teach a sharply delimited segment of the field or to range widely across it. It also may make a difference whether one is planning to teach a course or a unit explicitly on the subject or whether one is preparing only to add a death-related dimension to an ongoing course or unit. With due allowance for such different intents, however, there are a number of areas which almost any teacher should be familiar with, at least to some degree.

One such area concerns the elderly. To the extent that they can, teachers should become knowledgeable about the aging process and the physiological, psychological, and socioeconomic changes which accompany aging in our society. They should be aware of what the problems are that older people face in adjusting to advanced age and to retirement, the options they have and the options which are foreclosed to them. Teachers should have some appreciation of how conditions for the elderly differ among our various cultural and socioeconomic groups. They should also be alert to the particular kinds of mental disturbance that are common in later life, and they should be knowledgeable about public and private provisions the community makes for the economic security of the elderly, for their health care, employment, education, entertainment, transportation, and housing.

Much has been written on the problems of the elderly, but compared with the literature on aging, that on death and dying is massive, so voluminous that teachers can and should be highly selective. Choices, of course, will depend somewhat on the teacher's academic and life experiences, the nature of the course or unit he or she plans to teach, and the age and experience of the students. But whatever the nature of these variables, at least for their own background, teachers should be conversant with the major philosophic, religious, psychological, and sociological perspectives in the field. They should be aware of current thinking and action in such areas as grief and bereavement, death definition, suicide, euthanasia, and funeral practices. They should also be familiar with some of the responses to death expressed by poets, novelists, artists, and film makers.

As formidable as the task of understanding the subject matter may be for the death and dying education teacher, an equally important responsibility is understanding the students. Without that understanding, the teacher can do irreparable damage. The teacher should have a clear idea of the range of possible attitudes toward death the students may have when they enter the class, their reasons for taking the class, their sensitivities and insecurities, their recent as well as past experiences with death. Classes should be small enough to promote frank discussion and, when students are so inclined, self-disclosure. In such an atmosphere, given the nature of much of the course content, the death and dying education teacher should be alert to signs a student needs professional help that the course or teacher cannot provide. And the teacher should know in advance where that help can be provided, either in the school system or outside it. Perhaps because death and dying courses involve students at a deep visceral as well as an intellectual level and also because they

tend to attract students who have unresolved death-related problems, teachers should be prepared for their emergence.

So much for what the death education teachers should *know*. But
what should they *be*? Is there any distinctive body of experience
death educators should have had? Obviously they cannot have
experienced death, but they are better prepared if their lives have
consciously touched death and if they have reached at least a tenta-
tive position with respect to it. This does not mean that they need
actually to have known tragedy in their own lives, nor that they
have had psychoanalysis or psychotherapy. It does mean, however,
that they have lived fully, thought deeply, expressed themselves
honestly, and arrived at a considered personal position with respect
to the meaning of death.

Are there any distinguishing personal attributes death and dying
educators should have? Only those which distinguish all good
teachers. They should know their subject matter and their students
and have come to terms with their own anxieties about dying. They
should also know how to involve school administrators, parents, and
townspeople in designing, teaching, and evaluating their courses.
And, most important, they should be able to use the language of
death and dying easily and naturally with their students, to elicit
and then to listen to their ideas—to establish a stimulating, honest,
and supportive environment, one in which students and teachers
together can delve into some of the dark corners of one of our most
preplexing problems.

8. A Course of Study

> The result of the educative process is the capacity for further education.
>
> John Dewey

As every teacher who has tried one knows, a packaged course can provide a valuable starting point, but it invariably requires tailoring to meet the needs and abilities of a specific class as well as the goals and capacities of the individual teacher. The Amherst (Mass.) High School course which follows may serve as one such starting point for the secondary teacher who is planning a death-related course. Taught first in 1975 as a nine-week unit, it has since been expanded to an eighteen-week course; its enrollment doubled, from 60 to 120, between the first and second spring it was offered. Individual classes average about 30 students and include a heterogeneous mix of sophomores, juniors, and seniors. In the Amherst elective program, those who choose to take it as a Phase 5 subject are expected to meet more rigorous objectives than those who enroll as Phase 4 or 3 students and receive correspondingly higher academic credit for having met them. A syllabus for the eighteen-week course is provided later in this chapter; first the teacher, Robert Kelly, tells how he came to design the course and the experience he and the students have had with it.

(The course may be modified for shorter time spans. For example, a four-week course might contain A. Values Clarification and G. Comparative Cultural Views of Death, or it might concentrate on a single issue such as F. Grief, Mourning, and Counseling, after a short introductory phase of values clarification. Longer courses of 8, 10, or 15 weeks could cover all of the topics with the activities limited to accommodate the short time span. Naturally, the teacher is the best judge of the needs of a group of students, so the option of course design to suit specific concerns and interests is open to any teacher who wishes to develop a course such as this on death or dying.)

Teaching a Course on Death and Dying
Robert Kelly

Every few years the field of social studies experiences another "hot topic." In the nine years I have been teaching I have witnessed the emergence of black studies and race relations, environmental studies, law education, urban studies, women's studies, and now death education. While I believe that the arrival of these topics is long overdue, I think it's important to note that sometimes it's easy to treat them as simply fads or soft curriculum to sell to students in order to achieve "relevance." Given the cynicism that certain sectors of the public have toward such courses and given the quantity of materials—often mediocre—that publishers have produced to meet the demand, it's imperative that we educators proceed with some caution in developing these new courses of study.

The study of death is probably the last of the old taboos to fall in the schools. It's certainly not surprising that the subject should be one of the more recent arrivals in the curriculum, given Americans' distaste for consideration of it. Teachers resemble the public in terms of their discomfort, embarrassment, and general reluctance to explore certain subjects.

My own experience in teaching this course is limited to three years. I first thought of the need for such a course a number of years ago, but, primarily because of other curriculum commitments, I was unable to give serious thought to developing a unit. Admittedly, a secondary consideration was my own questioning of whether my high school was ready for such a course. In broaching the subject informally with my colleagues, the topic usually generated a few laughs and a few jokes (and occasionally some serious comments). Finally, I was not ready to develop another course from "scratch" as I had just done so with several other courses. At that time there was a dearth of materials—print and nonprint—available for high school students, and I wanted to have at least a base of some kind if I was going to proceed into an area of this nature.

In the summer of 1974, I received a brochure describing a minicourse David Berg and George Dougherty had produced called "Perspectives on Death" and the timing seemed right. I had my base, and also had had some recent conversations in developing a course on thanatology. I put together an experimental nine-week unit and offered it to 60 students in the spring of 1975. The response was tremendous in terms of interest and achievement. I refined the course a bit and offered it again in the spring of 1976 to 120 students. Again, the response was excellent. The main criticism was that the course was too short, and the criticism was indeed valid. I was trying to do too much in too short a period, and at the same time, was omitting some areas which needed greater attention. Thus, this summer I have expanded the course to eighteen weeks with the help of five "veterans" of the course who have read and evaluated materials and offered invaluable suggestions on "where to go from here."

At this point let me pose some of the questions that are frequently asked about death education and offer some responses to them.

1. *Why is there a need for death education?* Any curriculum should basically be a study of life in all its forms and facets, providing students with skills, attitudes, and information to take into the "real world." Whether we like it or not, death can be viewed as part of the life process. Every human being will some day have to deal with the death of relatives, friends, and in some cases, face squarely his or her own death. While acquiring a body of information and considering personal cultural attitudes about death may not make the reality of death an easy experience later on, it may make the process a bit less threatening, frightening, and overwhelming.

Death is a universal phenomenon; and yet it is a subject about which people have much misinformation. It is a reality that most of us try to deny; and yet many of us have great curiosity about it. It is time to confront some of our fears, address some of our basic feelings, and answer some of our questions. And, as some of my students have suggested, in doing so we may come to better understand ourselves and better appreciate the beauty of life and living.

2. *What are necessary qualifications for teaching such a course?* I'm not convinced that only a "chosen few" are cut out for teaching this subject to kids. Nor do I believe that anyone can do it.

I believe that the teacher of any social studies course must have certain qualities such as general intelligence, ability to relate well to kids, imagination, ability to communicate, ability to plan and develop curriculum objectives and activities, ability to probe students' minds and sensitivity, to name but a few.

In teaching a course on death, I have found that sensitivity to student feelings, teacher self-awareness, and self-confidence play especially important roles. For some students the course has been a rough experience in that they have had to think about things that they, like most adolescents, do not like to think concern them directly. They equate death with old age, not youth. At the same time, many of them have experienced death via the loss of grandparents, etc., and either because they were closed out of the process of grief in order to be "protected" or were too young at the time, they have serious questions and concerns. The teacher must obviously be sensitive to various situations, knowing when to probe, and when to back off.

As for self-awareness and self-confidence, it is important for the teacher to feel fairly comfortable in talking about the subject in all of its facets. Students receive messages from all the signals teachers emit. I think the teacher of such a course should have thought through the question of his or her own death. What does death mean to you? What do you believe? Why? This is not to say that one has to have all the answers and be totally at peace with one's self in order to teach such a course. Frankly, I have my own fears about death; and I don't look forward to dying. But I don't view this as weakness or incompetence, rather as an admission of my humanness. Death has been, and probably always will be, the chief mystery of life, regardless of our religious beliefs and the advancement of science. A teacher should accept this reality and not be afraid to share his or her fears with students.

3. *To what extent should such a course try to change attitudes?* My intention in the course is not to make everyone accept his or her own death. To attempt such a thing would not work. Human beings are too strong and complex to be so manipulated within the confines of a school classroom. More importantly, I think it improper for the teacher to insist on such a value; the choice is a very personal one that an individual has to make in the end. A few students have spent the entire course denying the subject, and I accept their right to do so.

A more realistic and proper goal, I believe, is to offer a range of activities designed to enable students to think about death-related subjects. To gain credit for the course they will have to have acquired some information, demonstrated some skills, and explained with some clarity their attitudes about certain matters. What the students conclude about death in general, their own death, and life is up to them. My major goal is death awareness rather than death acceptance, and the students who have taken the course have indicated agreement with this approach.

4. *Is it morbid and depressing to spend an extended period of time on a subject like death?* Morbidity is in the mind of the thinker. As one author puts it, to avoid discussing death is morbid. Whether the course is depressing or not depends entirely on how the course is

structured and presented and what attitude the teacher brings to the subject.

When I first asked my class this year whether they thought the course should be expanded, the response was unanimously affirmative. But in discussing the matter, a number of students advised me to structure the course in such a way that there would be some "breaks." They suggested that the "heavier" topics such as dying, funerals, and grief be interspersed with "lighter" topics such as music, art, wills, and insurance. Our school schedule also helps, in that no course meets every day.

As for my own state of mind, I never found teaching the subject depressing. Certainly, I would not choose to teach five classes of thanatology a day, but then again, I would not choose to teach five classes of law or U. S. history, either. I do not dwell on the subject as I also teach courses in law, crime and punishment, history, international relations, and current affairs and have obligations in those areas as well.

Also, death-related subjects are not always discussed in a somber vein. Classes have their light moments, and the teacher should be encouraged to inject humor at appropriate times. After all, the course is not about death alone; it's also about life.

5. *Can you really measure the success or worth of a course like this?* Admittedly, the dividends of such a course are probably more likely to be paid at some future date. One can measure information acquisition, skill development. Here we have some hard evidence. As to attitude formation and personal growth, I have at least suggestive evidence from papers students write, comments they make in class, and evaluations they submit at the end of the course. Most of our students are pretty candid in their course evaluations (especially as they are anonymous) and about 98 percent of the students have had very positive things to say about what this course has meant to them and, in some instances, to their families. In one case a student's mother read the course books so that she could better come to grips with the impending death of a terminally ill daughter. In another case, a student whose father died a few months before the course started began spending much time talking with her mother about subjects discussed in class. And then there are many other students who describe fascinating dinner conversations with their parents. While some parents are bothered by the ease with which their children talk about their own deaths, on the other hand, they are grateful that they and their children at least found something to discuss.

Finally, the interest and support the course has mustered from various fellow teachers, administrators, and members of the community, some of whom I rely upon as speakers for the course, suggest that it has had some success. All in all, the teaching of this subject has been a most rewarding and satisfying professional experience.

Syllabus for "Death and Dying" (18 weeks), Amherst Regional High School

Introduction

Death is a subject seldom studied in school and often misunderstood and unnecessarily feared by a large number of people. Although Edna St. Vincent Millay once described it this way: "Death, however, is a spongy wall, is a sticky river, is nothing at all," there is ample evidence that many people have a tremendous interest in the subject because it is a biological reality, a cultural phenomenon, a spiritual event, an economic reality, and a psychological process. Alfred North Whitehead has said, "There is only one subject-matter for education, and that is life in all its manifestations."

Content

The readings and media in this course will draw from a number of disciplines, among them literature and poetry, art, music, psychology, economics, cultural anthropology, and law. More specifically, you will have the opportunity to study topics ranging from Poe to Shakespeare to funeral customs around the world, from interviews with doctors to the spirituals of Black America and the tones of a requiem mass, from wills and trusts to the issue of euthanasia.

We will have some speakers from the community whose work in some way involves death—e.g., doctor, funeral director, lawyer, clergyman—so as to help answer technical or philosophical questions. Also, we plan to visit a cemetery and a funeral home to further enhance your understanding of societal values and practices.

Finally, it is important to note that while we will study the ideas, customs, and values of different individuals and societies, in the end there are some personal decisions for you to make. We encourage you to question different views and practices and develop your own opinions. We do hope that you will understand why different people and cultures believe and practice the way they do in regard to death so as to enable you to better appreciate the subject's relevance to you. We also hope that, like some students before you, as a result of the course you will gain a better appreciation of life and living.

Phases 3, 4, and 5

A. *Introduction: Values Clarification*

Objective: The student will identify and explain his or her individual views and values about death and discuss American cultural values about death—past and present.

Activities

1. Analysis of a series of selected short quotations on death.
2. Attitude survey (adapted from *Psychology Today*, August 1970, pp. 67–72).
3. Film: *Death Be Not Proud.*
4. Berg and Dougherty: "How America Lives with Death," pp. 43–55. Also, for Phases 4, 5: Stannard, "Death and the Puritan Child," pp. 9-29; Feifel, "The Fear of Death," pp. 16-29.

B. *Physical Death*

Objective: The student will explain the medical components of death, i.e., definition, functions of coroner and pathologist, procedures at death, and the medical establishment's attitudes towards death.

Activities

1. Berg and Dougherty: "A Doctor Talks about Death," pp. 3–8; "Defining Death Anew," pp. 9–11; "Facing Death with the Patient: An Ongoing Contract," pp. 12–26; "The Coroner and Death," pp. 27–30.
2. Speaker: Community Doctor
3. Film: *Death*

C. *Dying*

Objective A: The student will state and explain several theories of Kübler-Ross regarding the stages of dying and the nature of relationships among terminal patients, families, and medical personnel in general.

Activity

1. Kübler-Ross, selections to be determined. Also, for Phases 4, 5: Feifel, "Personality Factors in Dying Patients," pp. 237–250; Kübler-Ross, *Death: The Final Stage of Growth*, pp. 7–24, 106–116, 119–126; writing assignment.

Objective B: Given a series of case studies, the student will identify and evaluate the attitudes expressed by patients, families, and medical personnel in each of the cases.

Activities
1. Film: *To Die Today*
2. Film: *Dying*

D. *The Arts and Death*

Objective: The student will identify various values and themes present in art, music, and literature dealing with the subject of death and explain to what extent such values and themes correspond to his or her own.

Activities

1. Audio-tape: *Death Themes in Music* from *Perspectives on Death* kit.
2. Filmstrip. *Death in the Eyes of the Artist, idem.*
3. Audio-tape: *Death Themes in Literature, idem.*
4. Berg and Dougherty: *Selected poems and prose,* pp. 51–74.
5. Modern musical selections to be determined.

Optional

1. Feifel: "Mortality and Modern Literature." pp. 133–156; "Modern Art and Death," pp. 157–158.

E. *The American Funeral*

Objective: The student will identify various customs and procedures employed in the American funeral today and will also identify alternatives that are available to the public. Finally, the student will explain what procedures and practices he or she would want in the event of his or her own death and why. Relevant factors include: (a) embalming, (b) wake, (c) coffin, (d) services, (e) disposition of body, (f) other.

Activities

1. Berg and Dougherty: "The Question of Funeral Services," pp. 68–79; "The Panorama of Modern Funeral Practice," pp. 119–145; "What about Funeral Costs?" pp. 146–150.
2. Speaker: Funeral Director
3. Field Trip: Funeral Home
4. Film: *Since the American Way of Death*
5. Field Trip. Cemetery
   Also, for Phases 4, 5: Stannard, "The Cemetery as Cultural Institution," pp. 69–91.

F. *Grief, Mourning, and Counseling: The Psychology of Death*

Objective: Given a series of case studies regarding the aftermath of death and the effects on survivors, the student will indicate the courses of action he or she would take in helping the individuals deal with the reality of death in terms of loss, understanding, and gradual acceptance.

Activities

1. Berg and Dougherty: "You and Your Grief," pp. 56–57; "Some Questions and Answers About Your Child and Death," pp. 113–118.
2. Susan Selinger, "Therapeutic Funerals."
3. Speaker: Psychologist on death
4. Pincus, *Death and the Family,* chaps. 4, 7, 9, 10.
5. Filmstrip. *Death of a Child*
   Also, for Phases 4, 5: Feifel, "The Child's View of Death," pp. 79–98 and "Grief and Religion," pp. 218–233; Kubler-Ross, "A Mother Mourns and Grows," pp. 97–104.

G. *Comparative Cultural Views of Death*

Objective: The student will identify and describe several major beliefs, values, traditions, and practices of a different culture, not his or her own, explain why these mores exist, and what factors might cause them to vary from locality to locality.

Activities

1. Filmstrip: *Funeral Customs Around the World*
2. Speaker: on comparative religious views of death
3. Film: *The Nuer*
4. Film: *Dead Birds*

5. Van Gennep handout, "Funerals," pp. 146–165.
   Also, for Phases 4, 5: Feifel, "Death and Religion," pp. 271–283; group presentation on suggested topics.

H. Special Topics: *Euthanasia and Suicide*

Objective A: Given a series of readings and media on the subject of euthanasia, the student will develop and defend or attack a position on the following resolution: "Should any form of euthanasia be legalized?"

Activities

1. Paul Wilkes, "The Right To Die," *Life*, Jan. 1976
2. Bender: *Problems of Death*, pp. 43–81.
3. Film: *The Right To Die*
4. Excerpts from newspapers on euthanasia.
   Also, for Phases 4, 5: Downing, "Patient's Bill of Rights," *Euthanasia Educational Council*, pp. 13–24, 61–84; "A Fatally Ill Doctor's Reaction to Dying," *NY Times*, July 24, 1974; Paper/debate option.

Objective B: The student will compare and contrast several views on suicide, using these views to develop a personal philosophy on the question: What should society's values reflect and its response be on the issue of suicide? Also, students will be able to relate this subject, where appropriate, to the issue of euthanasia.

Activities

1. Bender, *Problems of Death*, pp. 114–125.
2. Downing, *Euthanasia and the Right to Death*, pp. 152–162, 173–192.

I. *Special Topics: Wills and Insurance*

Objective: On the subjects of life insurance and wills, the student will identify and explain:

1. The purposes of having such "coverage."
2. The options or types that exist and the advantages and disadvantages of each.
3. The factors that can be considered in deciding what selections, if any, of these coverages will be made.

Activities

1. Sample policies and wills.

    2. Speaker: Lawyer.

    3. Speaker: Insurance Agent.

    4. Berg and Dougherty, "Legal Aspects of Death," pp. 181–185; "Issues on Insurance," pp. 186–191.

J. *Final Activities*

    1. Review of attitude survey.

    2. Film: *How Could I Not Be Among You.*

    3. Selected handouts for future consideration.

Special Requirements for Phase 5

Introduction

According to the Program of Studies, a Phase 5 student is capable of doing rigorous academic work, including independent research, creative and analytical writing, and the reading of fairly sophisticated materials. Also, it is the belief of members of this department that a Phase 5 student should be able to demonstrate leadership abilities in classroom discussion and related course activities. Therefore, I shall assume that you are competent in the above mentioned areas and are willing to devote a significant amount of time and energy to the pursuance of the goals of this course.

Objectives

While you will spend a certain portion of your time working on issues and problems specifically oriented to Phase 5, it is imperative that you demonstrate an understanding of the basic components of the Phase 4 course, because much of your Phase 5 work assumes and depends upon such a background. Therefore, you will be expected to satisfy the basic objectives of the Phase 4 unit. Since you should be able to handle these objectives without a great deal of difficulty, it will not be necessary for you to attend all classes. Specific arrangements regarding attendance at these times will be worked out on an individual basis. When you are in class—as opposed to working independently on these basic objectives or the Phase 5 goals—you will be expected to make significant contributions to the class, exercising some degree of leadership where appropriate. Finally, there are a few Phase 4 objectives you might omit, depending upon the research topic you choose (see section III below).

Phase 5 students will meet with me individually at least once during each cycle in the schedule. At that time, you can make progress reports and I can make suggestions regarding your work.

The Phase 5 goals are broken into three categories; appropriate information and approximate due dates for each category are given below.

I. *Critical Analysis of a Book or Articles*

You will prepare a critique of a book or two articles related to the subject of death and dying. Such critiques should include a brief summary of the major arguments or themes and an analysis and evaluation of such things as:

1. Nature of documentation
2. Quality of arguments
3. Style and readability
4. Questions raised but not fully answered by the author
5. Overall usefulness
6. Other?

Length: 5 pages (approximately). Due Date: End of 5th week.

Possibilities:

1. Jessica Mitford, *The American Way of Death.*
2. Lessa and Vogt, *Reader in Comparative Religion.*
3. Carl Jung, "The Soul and Death."
4. Paul Tillich, "The External Now."
5. Walter Kaufman, "Existentialism and Death."
6. Herbert Marcuse, "The Ideology of Death."
7. Frederick Hoffman, "Mortality and Modern Literature."
8. Carla Gottleib, "Modern Art and Death."
9. Herman Feifel, "Attitudes Toward Death in Some Normal and Mentally Ill Populations."
10. Curt Richter, "The Phenomenon of Unexplained Sudden Death in Animals and Man."
    (Note: Articles 3–10 are all in Feifel, *The Meaning of Death.*)

II. *Experimental Project*
(Choose one)

1. Conduct a survey on student or adult attitudes on some aspect of death in which you develop a hypothesis, create and administer a questionnaire that reflects good sampling, and analyze and

evaluate the results obtained. The description, structure, and findings, including analysis and evaluation, will be submitted in the form of a 5 to 10-page paper.

or

2. Conduct an interview with a person who is employed in some capacity related to the field of death (cemetery or crematory owner, funeral director, coroner, psychologist, etc.). Interview questions should be planned carefully beforehand so that specific objectives are addressed. Also, a brief 5 to 7 page paper should be submitted in which you analyze and evaluate the experience in terms of the quality of the actual interview (i.e., were the objectives satisfied in your estimation?) and overall usefulness for you.

Due Date: End of 10th week.

III. Independent Research Project

Write a term paper (15–20 pages) on a topic of your choice (subject to approval). The general objective would be to choose a particular issue, subject, problem, etc., which interests you and:

1. Discuss to some extent any relevant historical factors which have contributed to the present situation.
2. Identify and analyze the nature of the situation, weighing the validity of evidence from different sources.
3. Offer viable solutions, if any and if relevant to your topic, reflecting the arguments developed in your analysis and pointing out any possible problem areas in your proposed solutions.

Your bibliography should be fairly extensive and a topic should be selected within four weeks.

This project represents a long-term commitment to individual research. In addition to the requirements noted above you might be asked to provide an oral defense of your paper before a panel of social studies teachers, to be followed later by a discussion with the instructor concerning the report, a defense, and a self-evaluation of your overall performance.

Possible Topic Areas:

1. *Cultural.* Research the concept of death as it applies to another society—past or present. Areas for consideration might include its specific customs, values, the place of religion, life after death, music, to name but a few. Analyze these factors in relation to broader cultural values inherent in that society. For example, if

the death ceremony is quite simple, is such the case of societal values in general regarding the importance of material goods?

2. *Philosophical.* Research the works/essays of a number of philosophers—past and/or present—in terms of their views of death generally and/or suicide specifically. Compare, contrast, analyze, and evaluate these ideas in relation to any personal definition of and attitudes about these areas. Writers who could be considered: Hume, Kant, Nietzche, Durkheim, James, Freud, Camus, Sartre.

3. *Humanities.* Research a subject such as "Death Themes in Art, or Music, or Literature," beyond the scope of those themes introduced in class. Analyze and evaluate the approaches that various authors or artists bring to bear on the themes, comparing and contrasting where appropriate. (A project on art or music lends itself well to oral presentation—to the teacher or the class as a whole.)

4. *Other.*

Due Date: End of 15th week.

References

Chapter One—Why Death and Dying Education?

1. "You and Death," *Psychology Today* (August 1970): 67–75.
2. Frances Newton, "Light, Like the Sun," *Reader's Digest* (March 1974): 153–157.
3. Malcolm Cowley, ed., *Writers at Work: The Paris Review Interviews* (New York, Viking Press, 1959), p. 139.
4. Herbert J. Muller, *The Uses of the Past* (New York: Oxford University Press, 1952), p. 195.
5. Jacques Choron, *Modern Man and Mortality* (New York: Macmillan, 1964), p. 14.
6. *Ibid.*, p. 15.
7. Kenneth L. Woodward, "How America Lives with Death," *Newsweek* (April 6, 1970): 81–87.
8. Alan Harrington, *The Immortalist* (New York: Random House, 1969), p. 21.
9. *Ibid.*, p. 24.
10. *Ibid.*, p. 9.

Chapter Two—Are the Schools the Proper Place?

1. Robert Kastenbaum, "The Kingdom Where Nobody Dies," *Saturday Review* (September 23, 1972):33–38.
2. Quoted in "Thanatology I," *Time* (January 8, 1973):36.
3. Daniel Leviton, "Education for Death, or, Death Becomes Less a Stranger," paper presented at American Psychological Association Convention, Division 12 (Clinical Psychology), Honolulu, September 2–8, 1972.
4. "Thanatology I," *op. cit.*, p. 36.
5. "The Meanings of Death," *Yale Alumni Magazine* (April 1975):12–17.
6. Judith Hawkinson, "Teaching About Death," *Today's Education* (Sept.–Oct. 1976):41–42.
7. Dan Carlinsky, "Why Learn About Death?" *Seventeen* (March 1975):62–64.

Chapter Three—What Should Be Taught?

1. Lawrence Kohlberg, "Moral Development and the New Social Studies," *Social Education* (May 1973):369–75
2. *Ibid.*
3. U.S. Bureau of the Census, *Statistical Abstract of the United States, 1975*, 96th ed. (Washington, D.C., 1975): p. 155.
4. Daniel Leviton, "Education for Death, or, Death Becomes Less a Stranger," paper presented at American Psychological Association Convention, Division 12, (Clinical Psychology), Honolulu, September 2–8, 1972.
5. Quoted in David L. Bender, ed., *Problems of Death* (Anoka, Minn.: Greenhaven Press, 1974), p. 121.

6. Maria H. Nagy, "The Child's View of Death," in H. Feifel, ed., *The Meaning of Death* (New York: McGraw-Hill, 1959).

Chapter Four—Aging in America

1. William Kessen, "Ambiguous Commitment," *Science* (July 23, 1976):310.
2. Eliot Wigginton, ed., *The Foxfire Book* (Garden City, N.Y.: Anchor Books, Doubleday, 1972).
3. Deborah Insel, "Foxfire in the City," *English Journal* (Sept. 1975):36–38.

Bibliography

General

Anthony, Sylvia. *The Child's Discovery of Death.* New York: Harcourt Brace, 1940.

Bender, David L., ed. *Problems of Death.* Anoka, Minn.: Greenhaven, 1974.

Berg, David W. and George G. Dougherty, eds. *The Individual, Society and Death.* Baltimore: Waverly, 1972.

Butler, Robert N. *Why Survive? Being Old in America.* New York: Harper and Row, 1975.

Cassell, Eric J. "Death and the Physician." *Commentary,* June 1969, pp. 73–79.

Choron, Jacques. *Death and Western Thought.* New York: Macmillan; Collier Books, 1963.

————. *Modern Man and Mortality.* New York: Macmillan, 1964.

Cowley, Malcolm, ed. *Writers at Work: The Paris Review Interviews.* New York: Viking Press, 1959.

Downing, A. B., ed. *Euthanasia and the Right to Death.* Plainview, N. Y.: Nash, 1969.

Feifel, Herman, ed. *The Meaning of Death.* New York: McGraw-Hill, 1959.

Freeman, John M. and Robert E. Cooke. "Is There a Right to Die—Quickly?" *Journal of Pediatrics* 80 (Spring 1972):904–8.

Fulton, Robert, ed. *Death and Identity.* New York: John Wiley, 1965.

Gorer, Geoffrey. *Death, Grief and Mourning.* New York: Doubleday, 1965.

Green, Betty R. and Donald P. Irish. *Death Education: Preparation for Living.* Cambridge, Mass.: Schenkman, 1971.

Grollman, Earl A., ed. *Explaining Death to Children.* Boston: Beacon Press, 1967.

Harrington, Alan. *The Immortalist.* New York: Random House, 1969.

Hendin, David. *Death as a Fact of Life.* New York: Norton, 1973.

Hinton, John. *Dying.* Baltimore: Penguin Books, 1967.

Jackson, Edgar. *When Someone Dies.* Philadelphia: Fortress Press, 1971.

Kass, Leon and Robert Morison. "Death: Process or Event?" *Science* 173 (August 20, 1971):694–702.

Kastenbaum, Robert. "Psychological Death," in Leonard Pearson, ed., *Death and Dying: Current Issues in the Treatment of the Dying Person.* Cleveland: Case Western Reserve University Press, 1969.

_____ and Ruth Aisenberg. *The Psychology of Death.* New York: Springer, 1972.

Kübler-Ross, Elizabeth. *On Death and Dying.* New York: Macmillan, 1969.

_____. *Death: The Final Stage of Growth.* Englewood Cliffs, N. J.: Prentice-Hall, 1975.

Leviton, Daniel. "The Role of the Schools in Providing Death Education," in B. R. Green and D. P. Irish, eds., *Death Education: Preparation for Living.* Cambridge, Mass.: Schenkman, 1971.

Maguire, Daniel. "The Freedom to Die." *Commonweal* 96 (August 11, 1972):423–27.

Manney, James D., Jr. *Aging in American Society.* Ann Arbor: University of Michigan Press, 1975.

May, William F. "On Not Facing Death Alone." *Hastings Center Report* #1 (June 1971):8–9.

Mills, Gretchen *et al.*, eds. *Discussing Death.* Homewood, Ill.: ETL Publications, 1976.

Mitford, Jessica. *The American Way of Death.* New York: Simon and Schuster, 1963.

Müller, Herbert J. *The Uses of the Past.* New York: Oxford University Press, 1952.

Nagy, Maria H. "The Child's View of Death," in H. Feifel, ed., *The Meaning of Death.* New York: McGraw-Hill, 1959.

Palmore, Erdman, ed. *Normal Aging.* Durham: Duke University Press, 1970.

Pearson, Leonard, ed., *Death and Dying: Current Issues in the Treatment of the Dying Person.* Cleveland: Case Western Reserve University Press, 1969.

Pincus, Lily. *Death and the Family.* New York: Vintage Books, 1976.

Ramsey, Paul. *The Patient as Person.* New Haven: Yale University Press, 1970.

Robitscher, Jonas. "The Right to Die." *Hastings Center Report* 2 (September 1972):11–14.

Rudman, Masha K. *Children's Literature.* Lexington, Mass.: D. C. Heath, 1976.

Shneidman, Edwin. "Orientations Toward Death: A Vital Aspect of the Study of Lives," reprinted in H. L. P. Resnik, ed., *Suicidal Behaviors.* Boston: Little, Brown, 1968.

_____ and Norman Farberow. *Clues to Suicide.* New York: McGraw-Hill, 1957.

Stannard, David, ed., *Death in America.* Philadelphia: University of Pennsylvania Press, 1974.

Stengel, Erwin. *Suicide and Attempted Suicide.* Baltimore: Penguin Books, 1964.

Sudnow, David. *Passing On: The Social Organization of Dying.* Englewood Cliffs, N. J.: Prentice-Hall, 1967.

Toynbee, Arnold *et al. Man's Concern with Death.* New York: McGraw-Hill, 1968.

U. S. Bureau of the Census. *Statistical Abstract of the United States, 1975.* 96th edition. Washington, D. C.: Government Printing Office. 1975.

Van Gennep, Arnold. *The Rites of Passage.* Chicago: University of Chicago Press, 1960.

Veatch, Robert M. "Brain Death: Welcome Definition or Dangerous Judgment?" *Hastings Center Report* 2 (November 1972):10–13.

Wigginton, Eliot, ed. *The Foxfire Book.* Garden City, N. Y.: Anchor Books; Doubleday, 1972.

Literary Materials*

Agee, James. *A Death in the Family*. New York: McDowell-Oblensky, 1957.

. Asinof, Eliot. *Craig and Joan: Two Lives for Peace*. New York: Viking Press, 1971.

Barth, John. *The Floating Opera*. New York: Doubleday, 1967.

Beckman, Gunnel. *Admission to the Feast*. New York: Holt, Rinehart & Winston, 1972.

deBeauvoir, Simone. *A Very Easy Death*. New York: Warner Books, 1973.

Camus, Albert. *The Myth of Sisyphus and Other Essays*. New York: Knopf, 1955.

_____. *The Rebel*. New York: Knopf, 1954.

Cather, Willa. *Death Comes for the Archbishop*. New York: Knopf, 1927.

Gunther, John. *Death Be Not Proud*. New York: Random House (Modern Library), 1953.

Lewis, C. S. *A Grief Observed*. New York: Seabury Press, 1963.

Mailer, Norman. *The Naked and the Dead*. New York: New American Library (Signet), 1971.

Morris, Jeannie. *Brian Piccolo, A Short Season*. New York: Dell, 1972.

Orwell, George. *Shooting an Elephant*. New York: Harcourt Brace Jovanovich, 1950.

Plath, Sylvia. *The Bell Jar*. New York: Harper and Row, 1971.

Rilke, Rainer. *The Notebooks of Malte Laurids Brigge*. New York: Norton, 1964.

Segal, Erich. *Love Story*. New York: Harper and Row, 1970.

Solzhenitsyn, A. *Cancer Ward*. New York: Bantam Books, 1969.

Sophocles. *Antigone*. New York: Thomas Y. Crowell (Chandler), 1962.

Stegner, Wallace. *All the Little Live Things*. New York: Viking Press, 1967.

Tolstoy, Leon. *The Death of Ivan Ilych & Other Stories.* New York: New American Library (Signet), 1960.

Waugh, Evelyn. *The Loved One.* Boston: Little, Brown, 1950.

Wechsler, James A. *In a Darkness.* New York: Norton, 1972.

Werkman, Sidney. *Only a Little Time: A Memoir of My Wife.* Boston: Little, Brown, 1972.

Wertenbaker, Lael. *Death of a Man.* Boston: Beacon Press, 1974.

* See text of Chapter 6 for literary materials for young children.

Audiovisual Resources

Films

Dead Birds. Contemporary/McGraw-Hill Films, 1221 Avenue of the Americas, New York, N. Y. 10020.

Death. AV Center, University of Iowa, Iowa City, Iowa 52242.

Death Be Not Proud. Budget Films, 81 Santa Monica Blvd., Los Angeles, CA 91029.

Death Takes a Holiday. Universal 16, 445 Park Ave., New York, N.Y. 10036.

Dying. Documentary for N.E.T., WGBH, 125 Western Ave., Boston, MA. 02134

Family of Man: Death. Time-Life Multi-Media, 100 Eisenhower Dr., Paramus, N.J. 07652.

How Could I Not Be Among You? Eccentric Circle Cinema Workshop, Box 481, Evanston, Ill. 60204.

The Loved One. Films, Inc., 440 Park Ave. South, New York, N.Y. 10016.

A Matter of Time. Indiana University Audio-Visual Center, Bloomington, Ind. 47401.

The Nuer. Contemporary/McGraw-Hill Films, Princeton Rd., Hightown, N.J. 08520.

Psychosocial Aspects of Death. Indiana University Audio-Visual Center, Bloomington, Ind. 47401.

The Right to Die. Macmillan Films, Macquesten Pkwy. South, Mt. Vernon, N.Y. 10550.

The Seventh Seal. Janus Films, 745 Fifth Ave., New York, N.Y. 10022.

To Die Today. Media Center, University of California Extension, Berkeley, CA 94720.

Those Who Mourn. Teleketics, 1229 South Sandtee St., Los Angeles, CA 90015.

Other Media

The Mark Waters Story (¾ in. videotape cassette). Public Television Library, 475 L'Enfant Plaza West, S.W., Washington, D.C. 20024.

Perspectives on Death (audiovisual package). P.O. Box 213, DeKalb, Ill. 60115. Included are *Death Themes in Literature* (cassette tape); *Death Themes in Music* (cassette tape); *Funeral Customs Around the World* (filmstrip with cassette); *Death Through the Eyes of the Artist* (filmstrip with cassette).

Picking Up the Pieces: One Widow Speaks (¾ in. videotape cassette). Public Television Library, 475 L'Enfant Plaza West, S.W., Washington, D.C. 20024.

Since the American Way of Death (¾ in. videotape cassette). Public Television Library, 475 L'Enfant Plaza West, S.W., Washington, D.C. 20024.

To Think of Dying (¾ in. videotape cassette). Public Television Library, 475 L'Enfant Plaza West, S.W., Washington, D.C. 20024.

With His Play Clothes On (filmstrip). Order of the Golden Rule Service Corp., P.O. Box 3586, Springfield, Ill. 62708.

A